I0756154

Praise for *Who Is Singing?*

"The author's winning pattern of question/response page turns combines delightfully with *readable* bird calls and colorful images, inviting young nature lovers to listen, observe, and gain confidence in the outdoors. This appealing introduction to familiar bird song patterns and habits offers a sort of *first book of birding*."

—Sandy Brehl, former licensed wildlife rescue/rehabilitator, retired reading specialist, and children's author

"*Who Is Singing?* brings a whimsical wonder to the world of birdsong. Readers will also learn about bird behaviors and habitats from both the engaging text and charming illustrations."

—Ken Keffer, nature writer/educator and owner of Wild Birds Unlimited of Bloomington, Indiana

"Along with the fun illustrations, Halfmann does a good job of introducing readers to the sounds and wonders of birdwatching. It is a great way to get children thinking about the world of birds!"

—Alicia Frances King, Interim Executive Director of the Wisconsin Society for Ornithology and host of the Environment for the Americas Bird Book Club

"Janet Halfmann's book encourages children to listen carefully. With its brightly colored bird illustrations and read-aloud bird calls, young readers and listeners will be able to recognize their feathered friends in no time. What a gift!"

—Roberta Gibson, entomologist, children's author, and former children's nature and science blogger

"*Who Is Singing?* highlights the bird songs of several familiar birds that readers may find that are local to where they live. Bird call *phrases* are repeated within the book, offering a great way for kids and adults alike to remember the different bird calls that they may hear. *Who Is Singing?* is a great introductory bird book for budding young naturalists and a fantastic teaching tool to use while exploring nature."

—Brooke Gilley, park naturalist

More Praise for *Who Is Singing?*

"*Who Is Singing?* introduces readers to the gentle arts of birdwatching and bird-listening, from pigeons 'searching for snacks along a city sidewalk' to a blue jay's bullying screams and a cheery chickadee. Ms. Halfmann's tribute to these colorful, musical birds will delight readers and encourage them to look up the next time they hear chirping."

—Rosemary Kiladitis, children's librarian and blogger at *Mom Read It*

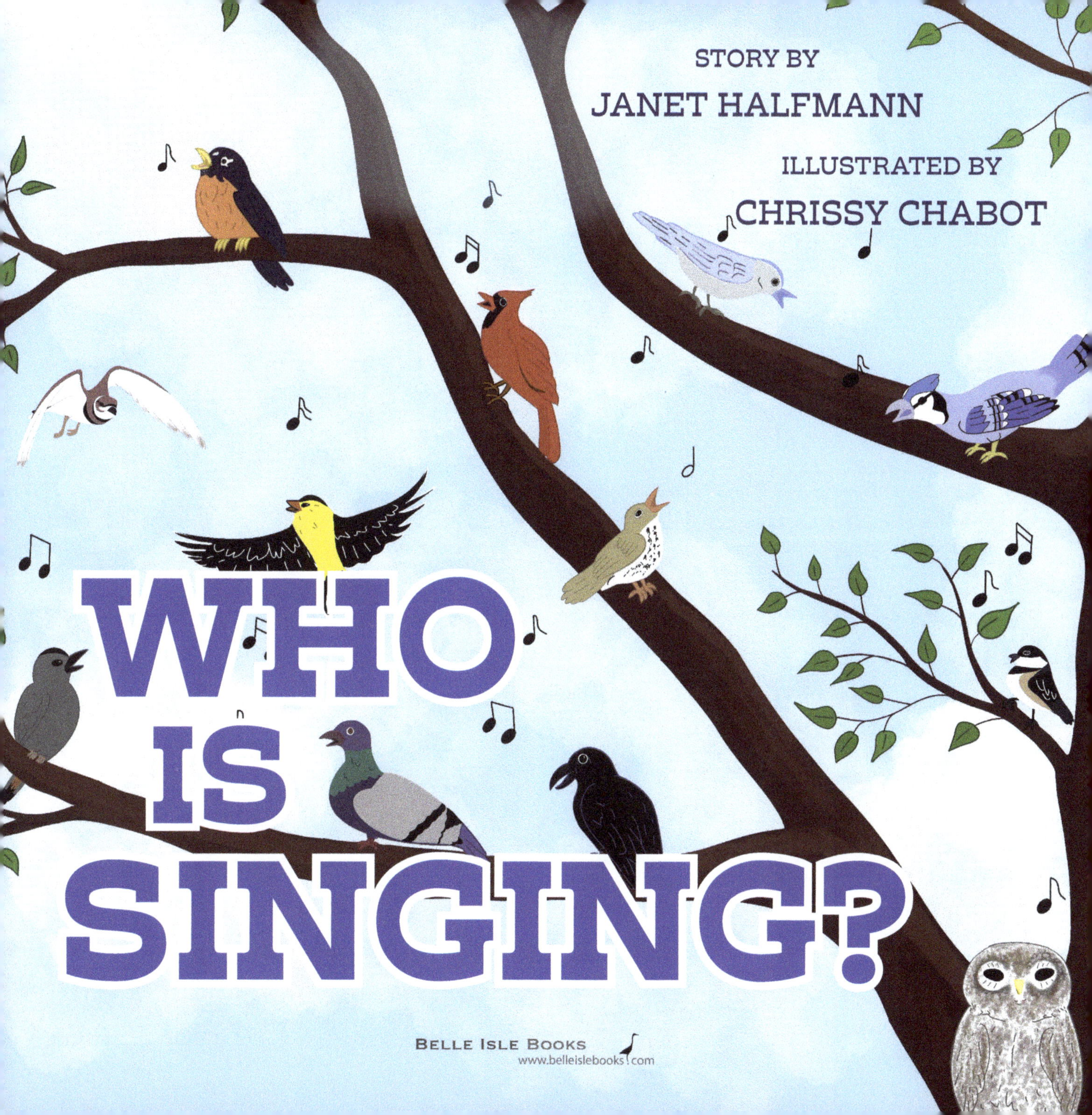
STORY BY
JANET HALFMANN
ILLUSTRATED BY
CHRISSY CHABOT
WHO IS SINGING?
BELLE ISLE BOOKS
www.belleislebooks.com

ISBN (Paperback): 978-1-966369-74-5
ISBN (Hardcover): 978-1-966369-75-2
ISBN (eBook): 978-1-966369-76-9
ISBN (Audiobook): 978-1-966369-77-6
Library of Congress Control Number: 2025927652

Designed by Sami Langston
Project managed by Haley Simpkiss

Published by
Belle Isle Books (an imprint of Brandylane Publishers, Inc.)
5 S. 1st Street
Richmond, Virginia 23219

BELLE ISLE BOOKS
www.belleislebooks.com

belleislebooks.com | brandylanepublishers.com

With love to my family—who know a walk with me means stopping and listening to every birdsong we hear.

Cheer-o-lee, cheer-up!
Who is singing?

Take a bow, Robin,
hopping on the ground,
hunting earthworms.
Cheer-o-lee, cheer-up!

Wheet, wheet, wheet,
birdie, birdie, birdie!
Who is whistling?

Take a bow, Cardinal,
festive all year long
in fire-engine red.

Wheet, wheet, wheet,
birdie, birdie, birdie!

Jaay, jaay, jaay!
Who is screaming?

Take a bow, Blue Jay,
a bully loud and bold
in beautiful bright blue.
Jaay, jaay, jaay!

Per-chick-a-ree!
Who is twittering?

Take a bow, Goldfinch,
dipping up and down,
sounding so sweet.
Per-chick-a-ree!

Meeoow! Meeoow!
Who is mewing?

Take a bow, Gray Catbird,
taking cover in a bush,
crying like a kitten.
Meeoow! Meeoow!

Chick-a-dee-dee-dee!
Who is chittering?

Take a bow, Chickadee,
all dressed up for dinner
in a black cap and bowtie.
Chick-a-dee-dee-dee!

Yank, yank, yank!
Who is tooting?

Take a bow, Nuthatch,
scurrying down a tree,
scouting for insects.
Yank, yank, yank!

Coo, ooo, coo!
Who is cooing?

Take a bow, Pigeons,
searching for snacks
along a city sidewalk.
Coo, ooo, coo!

Kill-dee, *kill*-dee, *kill*-dee!
Who is calling?

Take a bow, Killdeer,
keeping your eggs safe
by faking a broken wing.
Kill-dee, kill-dee, kill-dee!

Caaaw, caaaw,
caaaw!
Who is squawking?

Take a bow, Crow,
a clever corn lover
in a cloak of black.
*Caaaw, caaaw,
caaaw!*

Who cooks for you?
Who cooks for you-all?
Who is hooting?

Take a bow, Barred Owl,
hunting on hushed wings,
hidden by the dark.
Who cooks for you?
Who cooks for you-all?

Teacher, teacher, teacher,
teacher, teacher!
Who is warbling?

Take a bow, Ovenbird,
filling the forest
with unforgettable song.
Teacher, teacher, teacher,
teacher, teacher!

Birds are making music
all around us.
Listen closely.

Who is singing?

Fun Facts About Bird Sounds

- Bird sounds include calls and songs. Bird calls are short and simple; calls are used to signal danger, food, location, and more. Bird songs are generally longer than calls; songs serve to defend a breeding territory or attract a mate.
- The songs and calls of birds are their way of talking to each other.
- Birds sing the most at dawn and dusk.
- Male birds tend to sing more than females, doing so to attract mates and defend a territory. But some females, such as cardinals, sing equally well.
- Birds sing the most during mating season, from late winter to early summer.
- Baby birds learn to sing by copying adults. At first, the little ones babble, but practice makes perfect.
- Some bird couples, such as cardinals and barred owls, do duets together.
- Birds often sing or call from a high place, or while flying, so their sound will travel farther.

- Most birds sing during the day, but owls hoot at night.
- Birds have a two-sided voice box, which lets them sing two different notes at once!
- Some birds can sing with their beaks closed or full of food.
- Listening to bird sounds can make people feel calm.
- Some scientists think birds dream about singing—and may even silently practice while sleeping.
- Songwriters have used bird songs in their music.
- Besides the song or call for which a bird is best known, it usually uses several others. For example, chickadees have more than fifteen songs and calls.

Activity

This book compares bird songs and calls to fun words and sounds to make them easier to recognize. But not everyone hears bird voices the same way. Try coming up with your own words and sounds to describe the bird music you hear.

About the Author

Janet Halfmann is an award-winning children's author who strives to make her books come alive for young readers and listeners. She writes about family and community, animals and nature, and about little-known people of achievement. Janet has written almost fifty fiction and nonfiction books for children, including *The Clothesline Code: The Story of Civil War Spies Lucy Ann and Dabney Walker* and *Grandma's Window* for Brandylane Publishers.

Janet was formerly a daily newspaper reporter, children's magazine managing editor, and a creator of coloring and activity books for Golden Books. She is the mother of four and has seven grandkids and two great-grands. When Janet isn't writing, she enjoys gardening, exploring nature, visiting living-history museums, and spending time with family. She grew up on a farm in Michigan and now lives in Wauwatosa, Wisconsin.

Find out more at www.janethalfmannauthor.com.

About the Illustrator

Chrissy Chabot is a talented artist who has created vibrant illustrations for multiple titles through her work with Pen It! Publications, LLC. Chrissy lives in Maine with her family.

www.ingramcontent.com/pod-product-compliance
Lightning Source LLC
LaVergne TN
LVHW060634110826
845147LV00014B/907
9781966369745